The Rise of Giants

PART ONE

PART TWO

PART THREE

Partnership with Divinity

PART ONE

Joy: A Source of Strength from Within

In this fast-paced, ever-changing world with fleeting moments of happiness and sorrow, we're often faced with situations that tend to steal our joy, snuff the life out of our spirits, and give us woeful tales to tell. But in the midst of these things, it's highly imperative that we keep one thing alive.

There are things in this world we can't be guaranteed of holding onto for long (even if we wanted to), because we barely have control over them. But this one thing must be held fast, for it is the source of our living and the only thing that can keep us ahead of any situation that comes our way. I am talking about joy. It's beyond emotions, because emotions are tightly bound to present happenings and occurrences within and around us.

There is a thin difference between joy -- such that emanates from the inside -- and happiness. Happiness is often a result of pleasant happenings in a person's life; it's not always constant. Happiness is highly susceptible to change because it's a variable factor that changes with the circumstances around. So, happiness comes from an outside motivation, while joy springs from within.

Joy is that attitude sustained regardless of the present situation, whether good or bad. It's not susceptible to change like happiness, and doesn't depend on outward motivation for it to remain. This is why two people can be faced with the same challenges and situations, but still have different perspectives, perceptions and responses to their situations. Joy, unlike happiness, isn't a reaction; it's an attitude, a behaviour that comes from within a person.

How, then, does joy become a source of strength? What weight does it carry over our emotions that makes it able to keep us emotionally and psychologically strong, even in the face of daunting situations? The outcome of a person's life often stems from how he thinks, and not really what he faces. The Bible says, 'As a man thinketh in his heart, so is he'. This shows that what a person turns out to be isn't a function of the circumstances they face. No, not at all. It's a result of their response to those circumstances, which is based on their perception of the circumstances. What a man sees is what he gets. You can't expect bad things and receive good things.

Because the step you take determines what you get, your thoughts and the way you see things will affect whatever action you choose to take. This will, in turn, affect the results you get. Let me illustrate this using the example of two young graduates.

If there are two graduates who have been applying in companies for a job but both of them have failed to secure one, it's not automatic that they will end up the same at the end of the day because they are both facing the same thing. If the first man chooses to see it as a bad omen and recedes to thinking his life is an unfortunate one, that there's no chance he will get out of that situation or get a better, profitable job, his thoughts will invariably affect his disposition and his line of action, which are determining factors to his success in securing a job.

On the other hand, if the second man, although not happy about his present state, chooses to see it as a medium to improve on his qualifications so he can be better suited for the job and even a better one as the opportunity comes, he chooses to see the situation as a stepping stone to becoming better, rather than as a stumbling block.

When a man has joy inside, he becomes unshakeable, unbending, and resolute in his attempts to achieve success. There are situations of life that come our way to break our spirits, but the presence of joy in our hearts heals such wounds. See what the Bible says in Proverbs 17:22. 'A merry heart doeth good like a medicine: but a broken spirit drieth the bones.' Your mind has a great influence over your overall wellbeing as a person. Do you know that a person who believes they have cancer due to a false report or an error on the part of a medical personnel will develop the symptoms of cancer? Have you also observed that people are more liable to die of illnesses when left alone in the melancholy environment of a hospital, compared to those who are constantly visited and surrounded by loving family members and friends? These latter people tend to survive and even live longer.

What exactly happens? The state of the mind sends signals to the brain, which receives those signals and acts on them, because the brain largely deals with input. Just like a computer that only brings out what you give it. That's exactly what Proverbs 17:22 (quoted above) is telling us. It's one reason why ill news is kept from aged people, because the news could have a tremendous, negative impact on their health, since they have a weak immune system. This is also why those who surround themselves with negative things and hear negative stories often turn out to have negative events around them, because that is what they constantly feed their minds with.

Those who tend to think a lot pose a threat to their psychological and physical wellbeing. It's why we should always maintain an attitude of joy.

True, lasting joy can only be found in God. Because we don't have the capacity within ourselves to forever remain happy (as we're prone to focus on what happens around us), relying on God in every situation is the only guarantee to a life full of joy, free of worry and anxiety.

If there's one thing the devil seeks to do to every man, it's to steal his joy in every way possible; and he often targets the mind. He fills the mind with worry, fear, anxiety and doubts, using the circumstances around and the feeling of uncertainty. He knows if the mind is affected, then the person is defeated. And so, you must be very careful not to allow anything steal or take away your joy, because therein does your strength lie. Your joy is where you get the courage to face the vicissitudes of life and overcome them. It's that propelling force that makes you face each new day with renewed hope for as long as you're alive.

Rick Hanson, a neuropsychologist, said, 'We've got this negativity bias that's a kind of bug in the stone-age brain in the 21st century. It makes us hard to learn from our positive experiences, even though learning from your positive experiences is the primary way to grow your inner strength'. One of the primary ways humans tend to forfeit their joy is by focusing on the negative. The truth is, man is framed to focus mostly on the negative side of a situation than the positive, even if the ratio reads 10:90. Have you ever wondered why just one bad statement from somebody could ruin your whole day, which was initially filled with pleasant events? It could be a mean word from just one person, but it then turns to be your focus for the rest of the day, regardless of whatever good was said before and after that bad remark.

This shows that it takes conscious effort to retain the joy inside of you, and one of the ways is to focus on the positive, instead of the negative or ill-looking aspect of life. Most times, this negative part of life is often negligible compared to the positive side; but until you sit down and think over the positive will you appreciate and recognise its presence and effect. Unfortunately, it's the same thing that permeates even our society today.

The negative news is often the one that occupies the headlines of the media. No one seems interested to hear or say something positive. This is why you have to take proactive actions and be deliberate about sustaining your joy. No one else has that responsibility or will do it for you, except yourself.

It's Your Joy, Own It

Leaning on others to keep your joy afloat is a sure way to frustration and disappointment. When you depend on the responses of other people to determine your joy, you're only fixing yourself up for a roller-coaster experience of disappointment. In a way, you're indirectly giving unlimited access to someone over your emotions, your thinking, and your life.

Imagine having someone hurt you so badly and then you allow feelings of resentment, animosity or even hatred to rear in your heart. You lose your joy every time you see that person, hear their name, or think about them. The funny thing most times is, such a person might be ignorant of what's going on inside of you. Apart from that, that same person would possibly be living a happy and free life, ignorant of what's going on with you. So, indirectly, their presence or thought controls your own life: puts you under bondage and deprives you of your joy, because you allowed it.

Although you may deny it, only you have the access to your joy. You're the only one who can control, dampen or increase it (except, of course, you give another person access to it). No matter what someone does to you, they cannot steal your joy unless you permit them to. But some people don't have control over their spirit and emotions, and so, they're defenseless against any emotional assault that comes their way. Their guards are down, their defenses loose, and joy seems foreign and distant from them. If you would learn to keep and sustain joy inside of you, you must learn to control your spirit.

Although you have no control over what others do or say to you, giving excuses of others' behaviour towards you as a reason for your anger or sad demeanour is a sure way of losing your joy. The moment you choose to take control over yourself and not allow anyone dampen your joy, you're on the right path towards sustaining it.

Man is unpredictable and even the most trusted people in our lives can fail us. This is why joy is something that must come from within. There will always be someone who is against you, who doesn't like you, or who is jealous of your attainments and is seeking your downfall. All such will try to oppose you. Losing your joy to their actions will be a foolish thing to do. So, learn not to depend on others to make you happy or joyful.

Even when no one seems to be for you, focus on God, who is the true source of joy. He's the One who can never disappoint or fail us when we need Him, especially when we set ourselves in tune with Him. Every time an ugly situation comes in that seems to put you in a discordant state, remember to look up to God, the source of all joy. The natural thing would be to seek comfort in family or friends, but these are not guaranteed sources of joy. God is the only true source and sustainer of joy.

Apart from depending on others for our joy, holding on firmly to material things can steal and kill our joy. It's no wonder that many people who are rich, famous and even successful have no joy in their lives. We hear stories of such people killing themselves even with all the possessions they have, or committing suicide because of the dissatisfaction they feel. Pursuing material wealth and fame in an attempt to be happy and satisfied in life is a lie and an illusion that never comes true. I'm not saying that attaining success and becoming rich are wrong in themselves. No. If legitimately attained, they're good, but they should never be the motivating factors and driving forces of our lives, because these things don't automatically lead to joy. It, however, turns out to be an irony that the more these things are pursued after, the more the dissatisfaction and void they create within us.

Material wealth and gain should never be pursued as an end, but instead, should be considered as a means to an end. When a person lives their life based on their possessions, it's like throwing a piece of cloth in the wind and expecting it to stand. That's not possible. That's how it is when you measure the value and quality of your life with your possessions and allow them to determine your joy.

Jesus admonished us in Luke 12:15. 'And He said unto them, Take heed, and beware of covetousness: for a man's life consisteth not in the abundance of the things which he possesseth.' Those who depend on material possessions for happiness can never sustain joy because these things are fleeting and they can pass away at any moment. What then happens when you lose all of them? Will your joy still remain? Will you still consider your life as being of any worth?

Beyond what you have, beyond your state and status, let your joy spring forth from within. What will be left of you or said of you when your riches and fame and wealth are gone? They are outward, variable factors which are susceptible to change at any time, because you can lose them all at once.

To sustain joy, you have to learn to live your life independent of material things. This doesn't mean you shouldn't take them as important or valuable, because they are. Remember I said earlier that they are a means to an end. That means you need these things to accomplish your purpose, to live a good life, to be comfortable and well, but they shouldn't be the end you're driving at. They shouldn't be what your life is all about. There's more to life than what you can see, touch, and taste. Until you can independently enjoy your life without these material possessions, you've not come to the full realisation of what life is all about.

To get a dose of joy daily, you must cultivate the habit of focusing on what is good. Even the Bible encourages us to think only on those things that are true, honest, just, pure, lovely and **of good report**, as long as they are praiseworthy and have virtue. This passage, Philippians 4:8, is an antidote to any sorrow-filled, depressed life. It also emphasises the influence of our thoughts on our joy level. What do you constantly think about? What do you listen to? What do you watch?

These things influence your thought life and tend to either kill your joy, or build it and keep it abounding.

Why there's an increase in depressed people is because the form of information flying about is discouraging and that is what people focus on. You have to learn to look within and pick out those things that truly matter, and can have a positive effect on your life.

Winning with Gratitude, Hope and Joy

One way of practically sustaining your joy is to be grateful for the good things in your life. We often see the good things in our lives as minute and normal. We tend to overlook the wonderful things that surround us in a bid to be more realistic and factual with the world, but this isn't the best way to go. Cultivating a habit of gratitude for whatever good there is in your life will require you to think on what those things are. Because they are not always evident to us on the surface, we have to sit back, stay calm, and look into our lives to recognise and appreciate them.

Every day, after you wake up and before you sleep, make it a habit to think about what you can be thankful for, even the seemingly little things. You could also keep a gratitude journal where you write down the things you're grateful for -- the good experiences you've faced and the happy memories. It becomes easier to go back to them and refresh your memory when you're in an unpleasant situation.

Be grateful for the breath of life, for the family you have, for the gift of friends, for the power of love, for the wonders of nature, and God's creation. Just look around you and keenly observe; there are so many things to be grateful for, if only you would look for them. A heart of gratitude will never be put down even in challenging situations, because it's able to keep hope alive and express faith in seeing the light after being in a dark tunnel.

It also all boils down to perception. If you take the circumstances of life as a medium to grow and improve and be better, I tell you, it won't be difficult to always maintain a positive outlook, no matter what happens to you. It's what you choose to see that will become reality to you. Always try to see and make lemonade out of lemons. It may not be easy, especially when the circumstances around seem overwhelming and beyond your control. This is why God has to be your constant companion and confidant, the One you run to in every situation.

There are people who die before they are dead. What do I mean by this? When there's nothing to hope for, then there's nothing to live for. These people live in constant fear of the future. They are always afraid of what is going to happen, even before they see it happen. They take every kind gesture as a suspicious move against them, and they always seem to misinterpret things to their disadvantage. Even when today is sunny and bright, they always seem to predict the next day would be gloomy and dark and so, they are always in a constant state of anxiety, worrying about anything and everything. Because of the presence of fear in their lives, joy cannot stay there. Even if it comes, it's quickly replaced with fear. It's a pity that even when nothing is wrong, they live their lives in constant trepidation, bringing themselves under the bondage of unnecessary care and agitation.

Truly, life is uncertain and unpredictable. We cannot always define what's going to happen the next minute; things sometimes fall out of place even when we plan. But all these shouldn't be a reason for anyone to fret. Fretting never solves the problem (and that's if there is any); it only adds to it.

Most times, what we're afraid of doesn't even exist; but when we begin to focus on things and circumstances we can't control, our minds begin to create false illusions. Most people die more from fear and anxiety than what they are even afraid of, because fear has the capacity to elevate a situation more than it really is. Fear and anxiety are some of the main causes of health problems in our world today, leading to issues such as hypertension, high blood pressure, heart attacks and the rest.

Instead of focusing on events you can't control or change, why not pay attention to the things you can change and control? Jesus said in Matthew 6:25, 'Therefore I say unto you, Take no thought for your life, what ye shall eat, or what ye shall drink; not yet for your body, what ye shall put on. Is not the life more than meat, and the body than raiment?' Here, Jesus wasn't saying we shouldn't plan our meals and other basic necessities of life; what He meant was we should not allow the thought of tomorrow consume us and deprive us of today's joy. The fact that you are alive means there's a reason to be hopeful and full of joy. Learn to focus on the present, instead of worrying about what you haven't even seen. Don't deprive yourself of the joy today brings with the fear of what tomorrow might bring.

To have a daily supply of joy, you must learn to live each day at a time. You see, in life, all you truly have is today, because yesterday is gone. It's off your fingers. Tomorrow may never come, no matter how you look forward to it -- this isn't to say you shouldn't plan for the future -- but the present is what you're very sure of. It's what is right before you, what you can lay hold on, what you have. So, it's wise to do the best you can at the present, and leave tomorrow for itself. Don't fret about the future; focus on the now. This is one way to sustain and keep your joy alive.

Another thing is to always expect the best. I say this because even the present situation may not be rosy and smooth and pleasant, but keep a positive outlook, no matter what. Learn to always see the good in every situation; there's always something you can learn from any experience.

Marianne Williamson said, 'Joy is what happens to us when we allow ourselves to recognise how good things really are'. As I mentioned earlier, joy isn't something that jumps on us out of the blue. It's an attitude that we consciously allow to manifest in our everyday lives. When you make a decision to look within you, to look beyond present circumstances and to look up, you'd find joy filling your heart and radiating your life. The one who constantly sees the good in every situation will always experience good in every situation. It's an attitude that must be learnt, and it starts with your thoughts. It starts with what you decide to see.

Two people can be looking at the same thing, yet be seeing different things. That's what's called perception. It's possible that two people look out on the ocean. While one sees the terrible sharks and fishes lying underneath, the other sees the blue sea reflecting the sun's rays and showing the beauty of nature, and fishes swimming in the water.

Do you know what will happen to both, although they are looking at the same thing? One will give in to fear while the other will be filled with admiration of the beauty of nature. Not only that their perceptions will determine their actions. The first person will be afraid and reluctant to go anywhere near the sea, while the other will be more than glad to launch into the ocean and sail. Can you see what perception can do in determining how joy is established in one's life? What you choose to see is what you will get.

Russel Nelson succinctly brings home this point when he said, 'The joy we feel has little to do with the circumstances of our lives and everything to do with the focus of our lives'. You can't attract something you do not see happening. When you fill your heart with joy, you'd have a positive outlook on life and therefore, have a positive attitude that will invariably give you positive results.

If you can successfully keep a positive outlook in every situation and pick out lessons from the experiences you face, you'd be surprised how wonderful your life would turn out to be. You'd become an inspiration and challenge to others. This is because life in itself is full of ups and downs, but each experience is meant to make us stronger and bring out the best in us, when we respond to it in the right way. You see, it's your response that greatly matters in life's situations, and this is what keeps joy ever-abounding within you.

It becomes easier to appreciate that without thorns, there can't be roses; without the challenges of life, there won't be meaning to life. And this is what joy brings: meaning. Those who live joyful, fulfilling lives are those who have learnt to wade through the storms with the belief and hope that the sun will shine again.

'In everything give thanks' was Paul's exhortation to the Thessalonian believers. A man who himself went through various hardships, difficulties and persecution because of his faith and belief in God, he was able to give these words because he had seen and experienced the power of thanksgiving and appreciation in difficult situations.

Expressing gratitude attracts favour to a person. First of all, expressing gratitude to God shows that you acknowledge His goodness in your life. This becomes an imperative and a motivation for God to do more. It's why those who constantly express gratitude never seem to lack; they are often filled with more. The same applies to man. When you show appreciation for a good done to you, it opens the door for the person or another to keep doing more good to you. The reverse is the case when you carry a grudging and unsatisfactory expression when a good is done to you.

Imagine you bought a gift for someone with just the little you have, and in response to your good gesture, the person, instead of appreciating you, complains of how little or insignificant that gift is. What comes to your mind? What will be your reaction? First of all, you would feel bad and disappointed that your benevolence was not recognised and appreciated. Second, you would make the decision never to buy them a gift, to avoid such reactions in the future.

But if the opposite was done, you'd feel good and propelled to do more, knowing that the little you did went a long way to make the other person happy and satisfied. This is what some people miss out of in life, in struggling to get everything they desire. Favour is a deed done to you that you do not merit, or did not work for. Truth is, you do not have to work for everything in life. This is one way that joy through an attitude of gratitude brings favour to a person's life.

Let me ask you a question. Have you ever been drawn to a person's personality on meeting the person for the first time? Or, have you been repelled by someone's facial outlook even without exchanging words with them? I guess you must have. If you can remember vividly, what made you attracted to one and repelled by the other on just meeting them for the first time? It was merely the expression on their faces. The former must have appeared smiley and happy, while the other had a hard and serious look. There's every possibility that their facial expressions had nothing to do with their present predicament. That is, the smiley person might have been going through serious pain but didn't show it, while the other one had nothing wrong going on at the moment -- just that he or she chose to look that way.

That's exactly the same way joy attracts favour. When you're joyful, it radiates through your whole being. Anyone listening to you can tell the state of your countenance, even when they're not looking directly into your face. It will be shown vividly in your demeanour and your approach to situations, because it's something that comes from within. And when people see it, they'd be drawn to you. It will propel them to even do things in your favour.

No one obviously wants to be near someone who is always looking moody and sad and dejected; people are repelled, rather. How, then, does favour come? Through people. It's people that God is going to use when He wants to favour a man. Can you see how some people hinder their blessings by themselves when they are always pessimistic about everything?

When we drive away the people who are meant to help us through negative attitudes, we drive favour away from us. If you notice, those who are always cheerful are often surrounded with people. The atmosphere around them also makes those who are dejected and down to feel good and happy, instead of compounding their problems. Help will not always be far from such people because they are directly or indirectly affecting other people in a positive way.

A joyful countenance not only attracts people to you; it attracts the right people to you. You know, not everyone who comes around you is the right person for you but when you always maintain a joyful composure, the right people who always see life in its light will come near you. In this way, those who can affect and impact your life positively will be those who will come into your life, bringing favour along.

When you're full of joy, it will be easier for you to see things clearly. Your perspective about life will be clear. Worry and fear tend to bring a false outlook: an illusion of what is real and a deceit of what really is the issue. Your eyesight is, therefore, veiled and dim. They tend to blur your focus and pervert your sight. But a joyful person will be readily open to revelations and foresight because his mind is clear and filled with positive, enlightening thoughts. A joyful person is able to see things in the light of what they truly are, and able to make the right decisions.

Joy is your inner force of revelation and foresight. It's what gives you the needed enthusiasm to see beyond the present happenings, whether good or bad, and see what is ahead -- a brighter day. Your mind becomes open to the possibilities embedded in difficulties.

W. Edwards Deming says, 'Innovation comes from people who take joy in their work'. How true this is! If you don't find joy in what you're doing, you'd end up getting frustrated by it. Nothing will seem to work out and you'd always be finding issues with the process associated with the work. Have you found out that the best performers are those who find joy in what they're doing? Those who enjoy every bit of their work, that even when it's stressful and tasking, they find themselves going for hours on it? The trick is for you to work and focus on your strength(s).

What is it you're good at? What do you find pleasure doing? What can you do for days without getting tired? The answers to these questions are what should determine what you eventually end up doing in life. But unfortunately, many go for the temporal attraction -- either money or fame -- and then they end up being miserable all their lives, even when they have the money.

In a joyful state, your mind is refreshed. Your mind is the centre of your thoughts, decisions, intuitions, and perceptions. So, when your mind is refreshed in a joyful state, your intuition comes into full play and you can see opportunities clearly that are on your way, even in the face of obstacles. Isaiah 12:3 says, 'Therefore with joy shall ye draw water out of the wells of salvation'. Joy is what gives you the strength to face life and to get the best out of it. Make up your mind to rejoice always and remain joyful in depending on God as your source, and you'd see things falling in place for you.

You must be able to find joy in the little things of life: the birds that sing in the morning, the flowers that bloom at sunrise, the sound of the raindrops on the window, the bleating of sheep. Even the soft, gentle hug of a baby is a wonder that God has out in our world to make us joyful.

The problem only comes when we keep on getting busy chasing shadows, instead of focusing on the main necessities of life. And then, we lose cognisance of these things that God has put in place to make us truly happy. Spend some time to observe the nature around you; spend time to think of the wonderful moments you've experienced in life and take out time to thank God for them. Let your mind find pleasure in looking forward to better days and brighter possibilities as you go to sleep at night and wake up in the morning.

Spend time to make others happy, for therein you 'll find joy. Even if you have little, look for ways to make others happy and make life easier for them. Don't compare your life with others. As Roosevelt Theodore said, 'Comparison is the thief of joy'. Be comfortable with yourself while you make efforts to be better and you'd find beams of joy swelling inside of you.

PART TWO

Mind Power

Do you desire to live an above-average life? Do you have the desire to live a life of grandeur, filled with fulfillment? Are you aiming for the best you can be and do? Most people in our world today surely have great expectations and dreams and desires about what they want to become and achieve in life, but only few get to attain such desires. Why? There are so many reasons, but an outstanding one is because they don't know how. Or when they think they do, they actually don't. You must have seen people who work all day, working their lives out, but still remain average. (Perhaps, you've also tried your possible best to live the life of your dreams, but all to no avail.) This is mainly because so many people focus on the outer factors to get what they want, when in fact, they have everything they need within them to be all they ought to be.

The truth is, you have all it takes to be the best you can be, and that is what we're going to be talking about in this chapter. What is it that you have within you that has the potential to make you great and a giant in every endeavour you embark on?

What is that missing link that many people have failed to discover despite their efforts and hard work to make the best out of life? It is mind power. Mind power is the influence and power of your thoughts over your life. Whether you're conscious of it or not, mind power is the most potent force you have as a person to become a giant. Those who ever achieved great feats in life are those who understood this powerful tool that God has given to mankind, and made maximum use of it. They came to the understanding that their thought life is the most important aspect of their lives that controls every other thing they have to deal with.

It's no wonder that Solomon, the wisest man in the Bible, made this statement in Proverbs 4:23. 'Keep thy heart with all diligence, for out of it are the issues of life.' This verse indicates that everything you become, everything that makes you up starts from your heart, which is also your thoughts. Many people tend to focus on the external factors around them and they neglect the most important factor: their mind, their thought life. People rarely think or know of the great influence the mind has on the quality of life. It's often said that to change your life, you have to change the way you think. But why is that so? When there are many factors and circumstances that tend to intrude into your daily living, what significance does your thought life have? How can the forces of your mind overrule the external factors that seem to play out all around you?

Mind power simply means directing your focus towards a desired end or result. Take a few moments and consider where you are presently in your life. If you will patiently look closely, you'd see that your present reality is a result of what you've earlier believed, desired, or accepted as true. It's what we focus our attention on that becomes our reality. But most of the time, we aren't always aware of what is going on within us; we tend to focus more on what is going on around us.

Life is made up of energy, and everything we can see is interconnected with this state: energy in motion. The sound waves you hear, the light waves you see and the vibrations you feel, they are all as a result of the movement of energy. Even the thoughts you think! Yes. Your brain requires energy in the form of electromagnetic waves to function.

So, you can see that both the world around you and the world within are controlled by the same forces that God has put in place. And that's why what we think has the power to determine what reality we get. How possible is it for someone who's always thinking negative, always seeing the bad side of a person or a situation to experience something positive? The issue is, even when something positive comes along his way due to other factors, his negative thinking pattern will not recognise it as such and so, he will disrupt the power of that positive deed and use his actions to cancel its good effect.

When we think good or bad, these thoughts are transmitted in the form of waves which are interpreted by the brain and then the signal is sent to other parts of the body system to take action. So, when a negative signal is transmitted, what response would you get? A negative one.

In our minds, there are the conscious and subconscious parts. The subconscious part is the intricate part of our being; the part we're not so aware of most times, yet it's what forms who we are. The beliefs we imbibe from our environments and circumstances are being imprinted on our subconscious, most times, to our ignorance. And these beliefs lay deep in our subconscious mind, and they control our lives. They form images, sounds, scenes within us, whether they are true or not. One thing about the subconscious mind is that it cannot distinguish between the real and the imagined. It takes in whatever we give it hook, line, and sinker. This is why one experience you've had can affect the way you respond to other experiences you may later have, even if both experiences aren't related.

It's why a girl who was bitten by a dog when she was younger will have a high phobia for dogs, no matter how friendly and harmless they may be. She might even forget the experience she had years ago, but because that experience is still in her subconscious, she'd have this fear for dogs that she might not be able to explain until she sits back to think of when the fear started, or what might have caused it. This is also what happens in children who come from broken homes. Probably, their mother was maltreated by their father, or both parents got divorced. In later years, it will have a huge impact on their own family life and personality, even when they set out to live good and positive lives with their spouses. This is because an image or scene was created in their subconscious minds that wasn't consciously erased.

The reason above is why many complain about the output of their lives, even when they have made all possible efforts to make things work out right. But they fail to recognise the root of the problem, which is what has been implanted in their subconscious life from the onset of their lives.

Never try to change the external factors because they are often beyond your control. Trying to change that person's behaviour towards you, complaining about the hard conditions at work or the depressing environment you find yourself in, will not change the outcome of your life. You take control and take charge of what happens to you by controlling what happens within you. David Cuschieri said, 'The mind is a powerful force. It can enslave or empower us. It can plunge us into the depths of misery or take us to the heights of ecstasy. Learn to use the power wisely'. How, then, can we begin to harness this power to change our lives to our advantage?

What do You Want in Life?

As simple as this question is, there are many people roaming the face of the earth who practically do not know what they want. Their major aim is just to make ends meet, to ensure they are alive and well. But that is not what life is all about. Eventually, they end up getting frustrated for living below their potential, thereby becoming average and sometimes undervalued. There are people in suits and big offices making money and living big who also do not know what they want in life. They live life aimlessly; or even when it seems they have a focus, it's not headed in the right direction.

Imagine leaving your house in your car to a location without any idea of the street number, the place, or the city. All you know is you're leaving where you are to go somewhere. What will be the outcome of such a journey? If you started north, you might probably end south, or in the middle of nowhere.

Knowing what you want from life is the first step to living the life of a giant. It's not merely doing what's trending at the moment, or following the biggest wave of things or being at the spotlight of affairs. It's knowing what you're purposed to be and what you're supposed to be doing or achieving here on earth. I am talking about vision. What, then, is vision?

Vision is the projection of your future. It's what you see ahead of you, although it's not yet reality. It's what your mind is able to construe to be true, even when it doesn't exist at the moment. Vision is like a GPS (Global Positioning System); it's what gives you the roadmap to get to your destination and reach your aim. It's the manual you need to be who you are supposed to be and achieve what you are supposed to achieve. Vision gives you the idea of where you're going, not just where you were or are.

In creating a vision, it's important to note some things. Firstly, never underestimate the power of a vision. There are people who do not believe in envisaging their future. They prefer to take things as they come and live only in the moment without thinking of what their future holds. Unfortunately for such, they will be like a branch tossed to and fro with the wind, without any clear direction for their lives. They will be under the mercy of circumstances and obstacles that come their way. You may not have anything at the moment, but I tell you that a life filled with vision is a life with great possibilities of success.

With a clearly defined vision, you can move from zero point to hero point; you can move from grass to grace, from an average life to an exceptional life.

Secondly, never limit your vision. There are people who see their future with the lens of the present. They tend to streamline and limit who they are capable of becoming or achieving and unfortunately, they limit themselves. In creating a vision, don't be afraid to dream big. Expand your mind to see beyond the present and into your future. The possibility of such a vision being accomplished may not be feasible at the moment, but that is why it's called a vision. Just because you don't have the means to achieve it at the moment doesn't make the vision useless.

A vision is like an eaglet. It looks little and frail but when properly taken care of, becomes the greatest bird in the sky. There's no telling how far and high it can reach. The most important thing is to see it in your mind's eye, believe it, and hold on to it. Don't let your present state define your future. That's a myopic view.

What some people don't realise is that the future is in their hands, and that's why they tend to limit their vision. They think their future is a thing of fate, but there's nothing like fate. No one was created by God to be less than great in their own right, or to end up a failure. Everyone has the same potential to become great and successful and to be an achiever, but it all depends on the person. Another thing is to not let the opinion of people deter you from your vision.

Many of the wonderful innovations you see today where not thought to be possible years ago. But if those innovators had listened to what people thought or said, they could have limited their potentials and also deprived the world (you and I) of such blessings and benefits.

You can be anything if you can conceive it. As long as you can imagine it, you can achieve it. That's the truth. The power lies within you.

Thirdly, don't let the enormity of the vision scare you. Yes, you may not know how to go about it at the moment; but just hold on to it, as you will later see how the power of your imagination can bring your dreams to reality. With time, as you hold on to that vision, you'd begin to get a clearer view of it. It will begin to make more sense as things unfold. The processes you need to follow to achieve it will begin to manifest themselves. What about the resources to actualise it? Nature has its way of providing for those who have their vision in hand. The most important thing is to look at where you're now and prepare yourself for what you have to be. That is something within the range of your power. You can work on yourself. Ask yourself, 'Are there things I need to change or adjust in my lifestyle to suit the future I have created in my mind?' If yes, then begin to work on those things so when the opportunity comes, you're prepared and ready to take off.

Another thing to note is, having a vision as a roadmap doesn't mean the road will be smooth; there would surely be potholes and bends. But what vision helps to accomplish is that in the midst of those potholes and bends, you have a clear picture of where you're going. So, those things do not deter you or discourage you from reaching your destination. It's just like going on a journey in your car. There may be bumps, stops, bends, and a few hitches but will you then decide to turn and go home because of those? No. The same with life.

When you have a vision, those obstacles and challenges will only help to strengthen your resolve to get to your destination, not soften it. It will be easier to keep going because you know there's a place and a position waiting for you. Therefore, on the way to actualising your vision, be prepared for obstacles and challenges -- things that would want to frustrate you along the way. Just be determined.

Now, there are people who have an idea of where they are going but they fail to do one thing: to write the vision. See what God said in Habakkuk 2:2. 'And the LORD answered me, and said, Write the vision, and make it plain upon tables, that he may run that readeth it.' A picture of your future not clearly defined and written down is like a seed thrown into the wind to find its root and bear fruit. Will it bear fruit? No, it won't. Because it wasn't firmly planted into the soil. Although it has the potential of becoming a tree, flying in the wind won't let be in the right environment for it to properly germinate. And that's because it can land anywhere other than the soil. That's the same way it applies to a dream not clearly defined, detailed, and written down. It will have no root, no stamina to stand, no foundation, and then it is liable to die without actualising its full potential.

Bernard Haynes said, 'Without a written vision and a plan to achieve it, you will never live to your full potential.' And that's the truth. You won't be able to monitor or gauge such a vision. There will be no means to measure its feasibility; it will remain a blurry vision, not a clear, distinguishable one when it's not clearly written out. A clear, written vision helps to create clarity of purpose and direction.

Imagine coming into a city for the first time for an occasion and you need to find your way. It's possible the guest told you how the place looks like; perhaps, the colour of the building and other details of the location but even with that, the information isn't sufficient to direct you to the exact location. You'll need a guide, a map, or a GPS to guide you on your way. That's what writing a vision helps you with. It makes what you see more visible and realistic. You'd be able to determine the necessary steps and turns you need to take.

Doing this will help you coordinate your activities. This is where the concept of planning comes into play. You'd be able to plan your life in various areas in accordance with your vision. What you visualise won't just be an ambiguous term lying somewhere in the clouds, because writing it down makes it an achievable feat.

There's something that connects your mind and your hand when you put both tools into use. When you write things down, it's like an affirmation to your mind that that thing is true, feasible, and realistic. You may not know how it will come to pass at the moment but somehow, you're giving it wings to fly and soar on its own. Because by writing it down, you're registering it in your mind that you believe in its reality, you believe it will surely come to pass. Don't undermine the power of writing things down.

Another thing writing your vision plainly does is, it gives inspiration and motivation in the face of difficulty. When you're faced with a negative situation, the picture of your vision gives you something else to focus on, to look unto. It gives you hope that there's something better and bigger beyond what you're currently facing.

Imagine you were working on a business with the vision of having an international company that will meet the needs of people and suddenly, due to circumstances beyond your control, everything went down. You lost a huge amount of money; your clients went away and even your employees had to go too. A person without a vision will be at a loss of what next to do; they'd actually give up and not bother trying again. The fear of failing would plague and hinder them from taking a step in that direction. But when you have a vision, it will give you the motivation to start again.

With a vision in hand, you'd be able to pick up the pieces together, carefully evaluate where you went wrong and the possible errors you made, and you'd be able to ascertain alternative routes you can take to achieve your dreams. That's another thing about vision. With time, you can restrategize, rearrange and restructure your vision as things become clearer; you don't have to be static about it. You could widen it as you begin to see more possibilities and also point it in another direction as you understand yourself better, but not diminish it.

In the face of challenges, disappointments and hard times, your vision keeps you going. It's that propelling force that sets you in the right direction of your dreams. You can tell a man of vision from the way he reacts and responds to situations around him. You can't have a vision and want to let go of it, if you truly believe in it and its potentiality.

Writing a vision helps to create a balance in life. Vision isn't just one-sided; it's not something that affects just one part of your life, say, just your professional life. No. Vision encompasses every area of your life: financial, social, spiritual, emotional, and professional. Most people tend to write a vision of just their profession alone and that's why when they seem to be successful in their careers, their marriage life could be falling apart, or their emotional life could be in a mess.

When you're creating and writing your vision, make it whole. Let everything in your life be inputted into that vision, not that one side of your life is good and the other is on a bad scale. That's a wrong equation. Make sure you look at every aspect of your life and consider how you want it to turn out in years to come, because if one part is not taken care of, it will affect the other good parts in the long run.

With a clear, written vision, it would help you to wade off distractions. Do you know that it's not everything that looks good and comes your way is meant for you? Distractions aren't only about what is right or wrong, no. They could be legitimate and profitable ventures, but they may not be the best for you because they won't lead you to your destination.

A man without a vision can't distinguish what is meant for him from what isn't; he will be swayed by every opportunity that comes his way. When you have a clearly defined focus, it would help you to identify distractions when they come, and you'd be able to focus on what is right and best for you. It becomes easy to know when to say yes and when to say no to an invitation. You'd know what to focus on at every given time.

With a vision, you'd be able to tell where you are at the moment. You can't think of going to a place if you can't identify where you are at the moment. You have to know the 'here' before thinking of how to get to the 'there'. With a vision, you'd be able to tell your present state of preparedness compared to your future self and status, and it would be easy to make adjustments to prepare for that future, just as I stated earlier.

As you keep progressing in life, your centre of focus and measure of comparison will be your vision. You'd be able to know if you're making positive advancements towards your goal and gradually meeting up to the mark you've set for yourself. You won't be pressured by other people's achievements in life, because you know what it is you're aiming at. So, start working on your vision and start making progress with life in becoming a giant.

When you have a vision and it's clearly written down, it will be easier for you to let go of past regrets and disappointments. Perhaps you tried embarking on a task but it flopped. With a vision of what is ahead, you'd have hope of a better tomorrow; so, that vision keeps you going. You don't have to worry about what has happened in the past (the disappointments and failed attempts), instead, you'd be able to learn from the experience and think of ways you can become better, so you'd be better equipped for the challenges that lie ahead.

The mantra of a visionary person is, 'Keep moving forward'. A backward glance isn't an option at all; rather, it's only meant for retrospection and a way to take better steps forward in the right direction. You won't be bogged down on one spot sobbing, because the brightness of the vision ahead would motivate you to keep running.

Write your vision down and make it plain. Make sure when someone else picks it up, they can clearly see what you're seeing. Another reason for writing the vision plainly is for accountability. When you have a vision that others know about, you won't want to disappoint them or fall below expectations. With that visible vision, there's already a bar raised for others to see and for you to meet. I'm not saying you should begin to parade and announce your vision everywhere, but you should have a few people in your inner circle who will hold you accountable for your vision. People who have your good in mind and can push you when you're getting discouraged, motivate you when you're getting tired, and inspire you towards your goal.

Accountability serves to put us on our toes, so we're not slack in carrying out our plans. It becomes easier when you have someone looking over you, than just you alone.

A mission statement states how you're going to achieve your vision. Without a vision, there can't be a mission. A vision is the 'what', while the mission is the 'how'. If you don't know your purpose, how can you define what you want to achieve? How can you tell your mission, if there's no destination or driving force behind it? That's the concept of having a mission. Don't just write the vision; make a well-detailed plan of how you hope to fulfil it. You know I said you may not have the full picture of how that vision will finally come into place, but there will be little things you can do in the direction of that vision when you've researched and found out probabilities of what it would take to achieve it. So, your vision and your mission statements become the guiding rules of your life. They become the compass through which you sail through life.

Behind a vision, there is another important aspect: passion.

Passion, Gifts, Talents: Your Passwords to Greatness

We're all familiar with these terms: passion, gifts and talents, and although they are not the same, they are closely related. Passion, according to Merriam-Webster dictionary, is 'a strong liking or desire for or a devotion to some activity, object or concept. It is that strong desire that springs up within you for a cause'. When someone is said to be passionate about something, it means he/she has great zeal for that thing that can't easily be quenched.

On the other hand, gifts and talents are the innate abilities we have within us that aren't learnt or acquired, but which come naturally with us. Everyone has one gift or the other, and they differ with personalities. I can be gifted in writing, while the next person to me is gifted in sports. When a person is said to be gifted in an area, it means it doesn't take that person much effort to do exceptionally well in that area. He/she finds it natural and easy to do, compared to others.

Talents and gifts are the tools God has given to us to fulfil our destinies and purposes in life. Everything you need to become great is right there inside of you. This is why you shouldn't compare yourself with another, because no other person has the exact blend of gifts and talents as you -- they differ according to our purposes in life. The best you can do is to discover what those talents and gifts are and work on them to be the best version of yourself.

It's not always hard to identify what a person's passion, gifts and talents are. When you say you have passion for something, it will be evidently seen by everyone around you. Passion is loud. It speaks, it declares; it can't be hidden. Passion will move you to act, to take action. When you find you're passionate about a cause, it's often an indication that that's what you were made for.

Although passion can be seen, sometimes talents and gifts aren't evidently known, especially if you haven't taken time to study yourself. But if you will look closely, you'll find what you're extremely good at. You may not even know it's a gift or a talent, if it isn't something common or loud. You can discover your talents or gifts by asking those who have stayed with you over time and know you very well, like your family and closest friend. They will be able to clearly identify what you're exceptionally good at. You may also have to ask yourself questions like: 'What is it I enjoy doing best?', 'What do I find easy to do that others find difficult, boring, or insignificant?', 'What can I do for a long period of time without getting tired of it?' These and many more questions will give you a clue to what your gifts and talents are. When you do, pay close attention to them, for they are your keys to greatness.

After you've identified your passion, gifts and talents, that isn't the end. You need to harness those gifts and talents and feed your passion. They can be starved of their value and potential in your life when you don't take adequate measures to improve yourself and to use them. You need to work on and develop your gifts and talents. The mere fact that it's something you do naturally doesn't mean you can't develop in it. There's the need to become an expert in those skills and abilities for them to be maximised to their fullest potential, to impact others and the world around.

Many people abandon their gifts and talents and starve their passion, chasing after shadows or what seems trendy at the moment, and neglecting the very tools God has given them for their greatness and success in life. You may be successful but you can't be great and rise as a giant if you don't work and build your passion, gifts, and talents.

The Bible says that the gift of a man maketh room for him. It's your gift that would bring you before great men, not really what you studied in school. Making use of your gifts and talents and following your passion will require an act of faith, courage, and determination. It won't always be easy, but it will always be worth it in the long run. You must be willing to sacrifice, and put in time and effort to get the best from your gifts and talents. It will require sleepless nights at times, money for trainings, investment of time and effort for practice to be an expert at those gifts and talents, but it will surely pay off.

It may just be little steps of faith but just like the saying goes, the journey of a thousand miles begins with a step. So also, the journey to greatness begins with little, consistent steps in becoming better at your talents and gifts and following through on what you're passionate about.

When everything seems null and distant, how does the potent power of the mind bring your vision, gifts, talents and passions into actualization? It's through the potent secret of positive imagination and affirmation.

The Power of Positive Imagination and Affirmation

The power of positive imagination and affirmation is firmly embedded in the principle of focus. The power of focus in positive imagination cannot be overemphasised. Imagination has to do with what you see in your mind's eye. It's the image that plays in your head, although it's not seen in reality. Our imaginations are creative forces that come to reality when we focus intently on them.

The more we focus on what we desire, the more we see it. Why? It's because our subconscious tends to work on the images that are created within. Since our subconscious can't differentiate between the real and the imagined, when we constantly imagine what we desire, it will act upon those images and work in symphony with our minds to reflect and bring about its reality. If you want to fully activate the power of your imagination, take time every day to focus on what you want to achieve. Play those thoughts in your mind from time to time.

Even when your present reality seems to be speaking negative, change that thought pattern with a positive one. Your mind can only focus on one thing at a time. When negative thoughts seem to pop up, be conscious of those thoughts and exchange them with positive ones. With time, you'd begin to see those positive thoughts coming into reality. One thing about negative thoughts is that they tend to drain your cognitive energy, even your physical energy, and you can't be productive to even make any considerable progress. That's why people who think negative thoughts come out with negative results.

Take time out to envision what you desire to see happen in your life. The forces of your mind will begin to align with your perception and then, they'd begin to influence the forces around your life to bring about positive results in your life.

Another powerful tool is the word of affirmation. What you say is what you get. Even the Bible says in Proverbs 18:21 that 'Death and life are in the power of the tongue: and they that love it shall eat the fruit thereof'. Those who know how to use their tongue wisely will eventually reap the good fruit of it. The world was made with the power of words when God declared 'Let there be…'. We, also, as creatures created in His image, have the power to create our worlds through the words of our mouth.

Learn and cultivate the habit of speaking positive things into your life through the words of affirmation. If you desire to become a great businessman, regularly see yourself as such and say 'I am one of the greatest businessmen in the world'. You don't need to know how it will come to pass; just keep saying it and you'd see it come to reality.

Always affirm the positive and discard the negative. You can start with your vision statement and constantly say it to yourself, even before you see it happening. Don't be afraid that it would just end up becoming mere words. Say it and believe it. Keep repeating it, consistently and regularly. Meditate on it, let it become a part of your being, that you see nothing else than your dream becoming your reality. You'd be surprised how things will begin to work in line with what you've always been affirming and meditating on.

Also, learn to acknowledge your successes. Don't always focus on the negative part of your life. Think of the achievements you've made in life and the successes you've had; it helps to fuel your desire that you can actually achieve more. If you can put these techniques to work, you'd come to discover that nothing will be impossible to you. If you can conceive it and believe it, you can achieve it.

PART THREE

Partnership

'Just one great partnership with the right person can have an incredible impact on your business success.' –Janine Ogg and Jo Foster.

In life, we all need one another to succeed. We all can't make it on our own or just by ourselves, because we weren't made to live in isolation. We were made to exist for one another. There's little you can do without the help of other people. You need partnership to succeed in life. I tell you the truth that there's limit to how far you can go in life when you don't have the support of the right people.

What, then, is partnership all about? It's the collaboration of two or more people with the same objectives to achieve a common goal. There's nothing worthwhile done without the help of others. With the right people in your life at the right time, there's no limit to how high you can fly and how great you can become.

We'd be looking at steps to getting the right people on your side and partnering for greatness.

Value People

One way or the other, you will need people. The height you have reached at this moment is partly as a result of the people you have in your life, whether directly or indirectly. And in so many ways. Right from your birth, the nurse or midwife that helped in your delivery; the doctor that attended to your mum while she was pregnant with you; the teachers who taught or are still teaching you; the service providers of various services you enjoy are all a part of your life, although you may not relate with them directly. You may not even know them at all, but if they had failed one way or the other in their own responsibility, it could have affected you. Imagine if the midwife was careless with you when you were born; it could have led to serious damages. Or imagine that your primary school teacher was inexperienced and not efficient enough, it could have affected your education and reception too.

This is why you need to value people who come your way even when it seems you are way above them, because no one is useless. Everyone has a role to play in life, but some have a more specific role to play in your own life in helping you attain success and greatness. You may not acknowledge it now but one day you will, especially when you need their help.

People are invaluable tools that help us in fulfilling our goals and vision, and the truth is, we can't do without them. The more you value the people in your life, the more you'd see them come through for you in ways you least expect. And it will be easier to seek their help when you eventually need them. Imagine approaching someone you've ill-treated in the past for an urgent need of help. How easy would that be? It would take a lot of courage to do that, and you can't even be guaranteed that they would easily help out.

The person you're looking at as insignificant, little, or without much value can one day, become the person who is sought after by everyone. That is why you shouldn't judge anyone's ability or potential by their current potential, even if they seem not to be in the best state now. The tables can turn to their favour at any time. And when you see that someone in your life isn't living up to expectation, the best thing you can do to show you value such a person is to work on them; do all you can to make them better and someday, you'd be glad you did. They would appreciate you and you can't tell just how they might be of immeasurable help to you in the future.

Be good and kind to them and one day you'd see your kindness and favour being returned back to you, even if it's not from the same people. It's like you're sowing into your future when you help others -- you'd later reap it in kind.

How do you show your value for others to start with? Show interest in them. People know you care about them and value them when you show interest in who they are and their abilities. Getting to know who they are, what their life is all about and what good they can do or what they enjoy doing are ways to show that you're interested in a person. It draws such a person to you, as people tend to value those who show interest in them, than those who don't. When you invest in others and look for ways to make them better, they'd desire your own good and success.

When you're known as a person who values others, it will be easier to find the right people to partner with for success. They'd become part of the bricks with which you will build your wall of success. It will become easier for them to trust you with your own goals and vision, and help you achieve them. Apart from valuing people, there's something else you need to take note of: partnering with the right people.

Getting to Partner with the Right People

It's not about getting people all around you; you must be sure you have the right people. The right people at the right time doing the right thing is very crucial when you want to decide the people whom you'd share your visions and dreams with. You can't afford to get just anybody and say you want to partner with them without ascertaining if the person is the right person that should be with you. This is because getting the wrong person on board has the potential to kill your hopes and dreams.

Not everyone who is good is good for you; some people aren't the perfect match to partner with you. Getting to know the right people requires so many factors to consider before you make your decision. These factors must be properly put in place before you jump into partnering with anybody, because a wrong choice could mean a wrong end, aborting the possibility of your visions and dreams.

One way to get the right person is to ascertain if the person believes in your dreams and visions and sees them the way you do. If all the person is concerned about is making money out of the partnership, either they or the vision won't last long in the partnership, because except two agree, they can't walk together.

It's not possible for two people to walk in opposite directions or do two different things and walk in harmony with each other. There would be a conflict of interests. It could also lead to a clash of principles at the end. If the person can't clearly see what you're seeing, how then is it possible for them to run with the vision the same way you do? They will be pulling you back or slowing down your movement when you want to run with the vision. It will be hard to agree on certain things that require action in the advancement of the vision.

When you get someone who believes in your vision, they'd be willing to walk together and in harmony with you. That person doesn't have to be your family or your close friend, but someone you're familiar and comfortable with. It's possible that your family member or close friend may not believe your vision, not because they hate you or don't want your progress, but it can merely be because they are not seeing what you're seeing or seeing things the way you are and so, they don't agree with you.

A person who believes in your vision will constantly affirm it and even encourage you to keep working towards it when you seem tired and discouraged. They will firmly stand by you when the going seems tough, because they see the feasibility and potentiality of that vision, that it would be finally achieved. So, please, before you jump into having a partner or sharing your visions, be sure the person will believe in that vision.

Another factor to consider when choosing the right person to partner with is the compatibility of your strengths and weaknesses. Before you think about this, you must know your own strengths and weaknesses. What are your greatest strengths? What are your weak areas? Where do you often make mistakes? What makes you stand out? You need to answer these questions as a person before considering getting a partner, because in discovering your strengths and weaknesses, you'd be able to ascertain who would be suitable for you to partner with.

The strength of your partner should complement your weakness, so there would be a balance. There's no use bringing in someone who can do the same things you're capable of doing or who has the same qualities as you. One of the reasons for partnership is to fill in the missing gaps and make a complete union. That's what happens in marriage. The woman is meant to complement the weakness of her husband with her strength, and vice versa.

When this is achieved, you'd see the beauty of unity in diversity. There would be more creative collaborations and a touch of finesse in whatever both of you do. It will bring more variety and colour to your vision because the other person will offer what you can't offer, or bring to the table on their own. This is one of the great benefits of partnership. Having varieties of skills and abilities doesn't mean having varying interests. You both need to have the same interests to successfully work together to avoid conflicts. It becomes easier to work with someone who has the same interests as you, who has common likes with you. It makes things easier and you would find it easy to blend together over issues. Check out your likes and dislikes. Do they tally? Are they similar? They don't have to be exactly the same thing, but there should be just a slight difference between them.

When you finally get the right person, define your roles to each other explicitly to avoid misunderstandings later in the future. Let it be clear to the partner what he or she is expected to do and the role he or she is supposed to play in bringing the vision into actualization because the truth is, both of you can't be doing the same thing at the same time. Let the other person know what he is supposed to do and what is expected of him, and state yours too. This also helps to track each other's progress and act as accountability partners to each other.

With the clear, defined and fully set goals, you can track how fast and how far you are both going when you know your individual roles. It also helps to avoid conflict of roles, as no one will have the excuse of saying he or she doesn't want to do this, and the other wants to do that.

Respect of each other must be present in partnerships. You mustn't try to override or take advantage of each other. Taking advantage of the other person is like hitting yourself in the head -- you are the one to feel the pain. Respect, they say, is reciprocal. If you'd like your views and your opinions to count, you must learn to respect other people's views and opinions too. Learn to see things in the other person's perspective. Don't try to dominate just because you're the pioneer of the vision. Remember, you also need the help of that person to achieve that vision.

Learn to appreciate the other person's personal values and principles and also, to embrace their uniqueness as a person because everyone is unique and special in their own way. Even when you don't seem to agree with their own views, listen to them, get to understand them, then try to explain yours to them so you can both reach a consensus.

Before I go any further, I'd like to give the analogy of the ant on the importance of partnership. The ants are tiny creatures, but they achieve great feats beyond their physical strength. How do they do this? They collaborate with one another to achieve a common goal. In the ant kingdom, they have different individuals with their specific roles. There are the worker ants, that major in providing food for the colony and building the nests where the ants stay. There's the queen, whose main role is to lay eggs, and they have the sterile females. There are also the soldier ants, as we all know. The synergy between them is an attribute worth emulating. It's also interesting to note that they choose their roles by themselves, depending on their preferences. There's no conflict of roles, and that's one reason they are able to achieve so much and fend for themselves despite their tiny size and little strength.

According to Wikipedia, ants as a colony also work as a collective 'super mind'. Ants can compare areas and solve complex problems by using information gained by each member of the colony to find the best nesting site or to find food. Although the ants don't have as much brain power as we have, they are able to classify themselves into different, specific roles, work simultaneously together, and achieve the same goal. They are an example of what partnership is all about and what it entails.

There's a whole lot to be achieved when you collaborate and partner with the best and right hands in a cause and for a purpose. The results are often astounding because it's a collective effort, much bigger than just an individual's effort. So, get on and start work with your partner(s) and you'd be surprised how much you'd achieve.

Be Willing to Let Go

You must understand that life is in stages and that each stage has its own peculiarities and challenges. Also, in each stage, we must understand that there are different people playing different roles. This is why someone you were so close to when you were in secondary school or even in the university may turn out to be a distant friend or even an acquaintance, not because of any grudge or quarrel between the both of you, but because you just realised you two don't seem to bond as close as before. One of the reasons for this could be that the person has fulfilled his or her role in your life at that point in time.

The person that was of help yesterday may not be in the best position to help you today, but that doesn't mean you should despise anyone who isn't so close to you anymore. You could still need the person later on.

It might be hard to let some people go but sometimes, it's necessary for us to make progress. You might wonder how letting people go has anything to do with partnership. You see, first of all, when you're still holding on to people who you should let go of, you might hinder yourself from making the necessary moves that will accelerate and support your progress. Another thing is, the people who are meant to come into your life at that point in time to help you won't be able, because there would be no room for them with the other people still taking up space. You won't even be able to notice them or ascertain your need for them even if they showed up, because you're still holding on to the wrong persons. And so, when the right people who are meant to guide you to the right paths and to see opportunities along your way aren't there, your progress will be hampered. And it may be hard for you to move forward.

Letting those people go also gives you a fresh perspective of your present situation and where you should be. You know, the people you surround yourself with greatly affect your perception and thinking; so, if you're not with the right people for that stage of your life, you may not have the right perspective and thinking for the next level. It may not be easy, but it's often for the best. It might hurt, but you have to be mature about it and look at the brighter side of life.

Consider the people who are waiting to fill the gap to make your life better. You can also reminisce on the memories you've had with the previous partners and believe that the ones coming in will be even much better than the former. You know, the more you meet people, the more possibilities of greatness you can envisage and achieve, especially when they are the right persons whom you need at that point in time.

There are many topnotch companies recognised all over the world who were founded by more than one person. Two people came together to found and run the company, and it was a huge success. We will be looking at a few of them. One of such pairs is Bill Gates and Paul Allen. They both founded the Microsoft Company in 1975, after Bill Gates dropped out of school. Bill Gates and Paul Allen were childhood friends since their time in Lakeside Private school. Although friends, they had common interests that enabled them to continue together: a love for computers and entrepreneurship. It was the common interest they had that drew them close in the first place, and also sustained them from being best friends to business partners. And they remained friends, apart from a little hitch between them before Paul Allen's death from cancer.

Another partnership is that of the founders and owners of Google, Larry Page and Sergey Brin. Google was founded in the year 1988 by this duo. Unlike Bill Gates and Paul Allen, Larry Page and Sergey Brin didn't get to know each other from the onset of their lives. They met while they were studying for PhD in Computer Science at the University of Stanford. They both invented Google's PageRank algorithm, Alphabet (Google's parent company) in 2015, which also includes Nest, Calico, and other entities in-between. At first when they met, they had some arguments but their common interest was their love for computers from an early age, and the fact that their parents both were professors. Also, they had a common passion for data mining and that kept them together, having similar visions.

Another partnership that shows the importance of how one person's strength can complement the other person's weakness is that of Steve Jobs and Steve Wozniak, the founders of Apple Inc., founded in 1976. Wozniak had a love for analytics, while Jobs had a knack for business and seeing business opportunities. In an interview with the Seattle Times, Wozniak said, 'I was just doing something I was very good at, and the thing that I was good at turned out to be the thing that was going to change the world.'

'Steve was very complimentary, and not similar to me. I had a lot of values about disdaining money. I had the computer skills, the engineering skills. Steve had the electronic knowledge, to a decent degree. He could understand us (engineers), but he couldn't design things. He hung on the marketing principles -- how things look to the eye, that kind of beauty, the Apple II -- into a product.'

You can see that what brought these partners together to achieve great feats in technologies that have changed the world is that they had common interests at hand and goals in mind. These are what kept them going despite unique personalities.

They obviously had things that weren't common among them, but they learnt to focus on what they had in common between them and centred on them.

You may not be a perfect match enough to be called partners but as long as you have common interests that help you work towards the same goal, then you're good to go. There may be disagreements along the way but if you both still have the same interests and goal in mind, those disagreements can be easily resolved. But when there is the problem of conflicting goals and interests, it's better to call the partnership off. This is where the aspect of letting go comes into play.

Communication

The most crucial factor that keeps a partnership going is communication. Without communication between the partners, that partnership is nearing a cliff fall. No relationship can thrive without communication. Communication is what makes any partnership to thrive! Effective communication must be put in place to ensure that both parties are carried along and that there are no misunderstandings lying between them.

Before making decisions on your part, it's necessary to let the other person know and be fully aware of whatever decisions you're planning to take, so they wouldn't be left in the dark. If not, that could lead to tension between both parties. When conflicts arise, it's essential that you both adopt the right communication tools to listen to each other and gain understanding into each other's views, as you try to find a solution and reach a consensus.

Trust

In a partnership or relationship, it's important to uphold trust between each other. Where there is a lack of trust, it could create serious issues of suspicion, which could kill the vision. There must be a high level of trust for two or more people to work effectively together, and this is something you must strive to achieve when entering a partnership with someone.

Trust is built over time by a person's action and credibility, also from recommendations from other people. Without trust, that partnership is like a house built on a sandy foundation; it may stand for a while but in the nick of time when fiery storms beat against it, it's caving in. Trust can hamper the survival of a partnership/relationship in the actualization of a vision. Trust, when lost, is often hard to regain. It might take a long time to regain that trust and that's why you must be careful when dealing with people in every area of life, not to break their trust.

The Law of Patience and Kindness

'What you sow is what you will reap' is a universal truth in the world. Patience, according to Merriam-Webster dictionary, is 'manifesting forbearance under provocation or strain'. It's also defined as 'steadfastness despite opposition, difficulty, or adversity'.

Patience is needed for you to achieve your goals in life. This is because what you desire may not come as early as you think; this is where patience is highly required. It also takes patience to endure the hardships, challenges, obstacles and difficulties you're likely to meet on the way to achieving your vision. The temptation will come for you to give up or give in, but patience gives you that doggedness to wait till the final minute. Patience is a virtue that has to be cultivated and worked on. It requires perseverance, hope, and some level of guts to wait for the fulfillment of your goals and vision.

Patience is also needed when dealing with people. Remember we're talking about partnership here. There are people whom you may partner with who may not be moving at the same pace as you. It may not necessary be laziness; it could be their nature or other circumstances stepping in. Patience is required in dealing with such people, so you won't miss out on the best they have to offer. It may require you motivating them, pushing them to give in their best, and continuing despite challenging situations.

Patience with people is another way of showing that you care and value them, and this helps to foster the partnership towards the actualization of your vision.

Patience also requires that even though you're not happy with your present situation, you keep a hopeful stance while working on your vision. The diligence needed to actualise and work towards your vision can only be cultivated through the virtue of patience.

The virtue of patience is needed to cultivate your talents and gifts to yield great results. Without patience, it will be hard to achieve anything worthwhile with your gifts and talents, because it requires consistent practice to become a master at your art. Results will not come immediately, so you need patience to keep working on them; you need patience to put in time and effort even when it seems no improvement is being made.

Patience will also enable you to go through the rigours and hard work you'd have to face in developing those gifts and talents. Nothing good and substantial ever came easy. Patience is just that tool you need to pull through to your desired results. Many people lack the patience to go through such processes; hence, they end up settling for average lives below their potentials and innate abilities, to their disadvantage.

Lack of patience is also the reason some people decide to take short cuts to success but unfortunately, could end up cutting their lives, dreams and visions short in the long run. The road will surely not be easy; you need patience to keep you going. Patience helps to fuel your zeal for your vision. When zeal is lost, there is no propensity to keep moving. Even when the vision is in hand, you might find it hard to move forward at that moment.

Patience is what comes into play to keep us going and to help us recover our zeal. A Chinese proverb says, 'One moment of patience may ward off great disaster. One moment of impatience may ruin a whole life'. Many missed their chances in life because they did not have the patience to wait to the end, so when the reward came knocking, they were nowhere to be found. They abandoned their visions and dreams and unfortunately, someone else picked them up and used them.

It's like the story told of a man who was living on a diamond mine. He was told about it and he began to dig and dig. He dug and dug, but all to no avail. Eventually, he decided to sell the piece of land to get some money to feed himself and his family. Guess what? The person he sold the house to didn't make much efforts before getting the diamonds that were buried on the land. So, invariably, the second man actually reaped from the labour of the first man, all because the first man wasn't patient enough. If he had waited a little longer and continued, he could have discovered those diamonds and changed his life forever.

Some people give up when they are about reaching the peak of their lives. Their lack of patience costs them more than the price it could have taken them to wait, which is no price compared to what they would get, whether working remotely or not.

Patience keeps you from the mistake of making hasty decisions in the heat of the problem, or the pressure of the situation at hand. In partnering, there are decisions that need to be made and if they are made in haste, they could lead to costly mistakes. Patience gives you the liberty to think things through and see people and things for who or what they truly are. Without patience in the world, there would be chaos and confusion because people would just take decisions at the spur of the moment, without considering the repercussions behind those results. But when patience is imbibed, it's easier to see the clearer picture of the situation, take the necessary steps, and find the best way to tackle the problem.

Even in the planning and implementation of your goals and vision, you should be patient enough to sit down and think things through -- not that you'd rush to write just anything, which might not be feasible.

Kindness is an act of doing good deeds to others. Remember I said it's like sowing and reaping; what you sow is what you'll reap. When you sow good deeds to others' lives, in no time at all, as you're consistent with it, you'd begin to reap the dividends. One good turn deserves another. It will surely be repaid back to you, most times, when you least expect it.

Sometimes, your kind deeds may look like they are not being appreciated or even noticed, but to be noticed shouldn't be the motive behind your kindness. It should be done out of a heart to see people smile, and the reward will come to you. Be always open to offer a kind word or do a kind deed to someone who needs it. Patience and kindness both require courage and strength. It takes dogged determination to practise them. Many men have changed their status for the better all because of the seeds of patience and kindness they had sown, which later brought fruit for them in the future.

There's one partnership I'd love to introduce to you.

Partnership with Divinity

You can't fully attain your potentials without the power and help of Divinity. God is the source of all wisdom, (which we need), the One who gives us the vision we have, who has implanted it on the table of the heart. When you need wisdom, which will be needed in the fulfillment of your vision, you can always ask God. God is the maker of purpose, the One who ordained every man for what he ought to achieve and fulfil in life. This is why we need to acknowledge God in all visions and plans, because He alone has the utmost say.

You can't partner with God and end up wrong. One thing about partnership with God is that He knows the way to our destination and He has promised to provide guidance and direction to those who trust Him for it. If you go about your life not putting God in your plans, your efforts could be futile at the end of the day.

'Trust in the Lord with all your heart, and lean not on your own understanding. In all your ways acknowledge Him, And He shall direct your paths', is what is written in Proverbs 3:5,6. There's untold wisdom in partnering with God on life's road. He knows the end of the journey even before the beginning. We need to depend on Him in every situation of life we face.

He's also the One who drops the vision in our hearts. Remember the verse in Habakkuk where the prophet was asked to write the vision down and make it plain? It shows that God is the giver of vision and since He knows the end, He also knows how to get us there. He knows the way, the direction and the route that are the best for the journey to purpose and fulfillment. Also, when you're in partnership with God, it would be easy to seek His help when you're faced with challenges that you can't control. These things will come, but God has promised never to leave or forsake us.

Whatever plans you have, whatever dreams you've envisaged and have written down as vision and mission statements, commit them all into God's hands. One other thing He does when we partner with Him is that He warns us of impending danger on our way. He reveals to us potholes that may be on our way, so we can take necessary precautions.

With God by your side, you have all it takes to rise to be a giant. You have the mind power and will to effectively spurn evil for your own good. The power lies within you to create the future you desire. Don't forget that what you consistently focus on will turn to reality; so, take control of your thought life and be careful what you feed it with. Speak positive words of affirmation to yourself each day, or as often as you can. Do everything possible to eliminate the negative thoughts from your thought process. Be good and considerate to others. Do these things and you'd find that you're already a giant.